KRIS KRISTOFFERSON BIOGRAPHY:

The Voice Of A Generation

Patrick Glass

Kris Kristofferson

Disclaimer:

The following book is for entertainment and informational purposes only.The stories, events, and dialogue recreated in this biography are based on extensive research, interviews, and the author's own interpretation of the available information.

Kris Kristofferson

TABLE OF CONTENTS

Kris Kristofferson

INTRODUCTION

Nashville was hot in summer 1971, but the air was full of excitement. There were a lot of people in the Ryman Auditorium, which is known as the "Mother Church of Country Music." Fans from all walks of life came together after hearing about a new country music star who was changing the rules. Then a tall, rough figure walked onto the stage, getting everyone's attention before he even spoke. Kris Kristofferson stood there with his guitar in his hand, looking around at everyone. At 35 years old, he wasn't a fresh-faced newbie. He had lived many lives before he found his true calling. A Rhodes Scholar, an Army captain, and a janitor at Columbia Records were just a few of the things that the crowd knew about him. But tonight, they were here to see the start of a tale. When he played the first notes of "Me and Bobby McGee," the crowd leaned in close and was mesmerized. His voice, rough and gravelly, held the weight of his life, and every word was true to himself. Janis Joplin had already made the song a hit, but the person who wrote it gave it new life. Kristofferson wasn't just performing; he was baring his soul, inviting the audience into the world he'd created with pen and guitar.

 The night unfolded like a tapestry of American life, woven through Kristofferson's words. He sang of drifters and dreamers, of love found and lost, of the struggles and triumphs that defined an age. With "Sunday Mornin' Comin' Down," he painted a vivid picture of loneliness and regret that resonated strongly with the crowd. As he crooned "Help Me Make It Through the Night," couples in the crowd drew closer, feeling the tender plea in every note. But it wasn't just Kristofferson's music that held the crowd spellbound. Between songs, he shared snippets of his journey—tales of his time as a helicopter pilot, of scrubbing floors while dreaming of fame, and of the nights spent crafting lyrics that would change the face of country music. His words, spoken with the same poetic grace that infused his songs, bridged the gap between performer and audience, making each person feel as if they were having a private chat with an old friend. As the night wore on, the energy in the Ryman continued to build. Kristofferson's performance was more than just a showcase of his skills; it was a testament to the power of perseverance and the magic that happens when authenticity meets artistry. The crowd, a mix of traditional country fans and younger listeners drawn to Kristofferson's outlaw appeal, found common ground in the universal themes of his music.

 The highlight of the evening came when Kristofferson presented a new song, one that would become an anthem for generations to come. As the opening words of "Why Me, Lord?" filled the auditorium, a hush fell over the crowd. The raw vulnerability in Kristofferson's voice as he questioned his own worthiness touched something deep within each viewer. It was a moment of collective introspection, a reminder of the human situation that united everyone present. As the final notes faded away, there was a beat of silence before the crowd erupted into thunderous applause. Kristofferson stood there, humbled by the reaction, a slight smile playing on his lips. In that moment, it was clear to everyone present that they had watched something extraordinary—the emergence of a voice that would help define American music for decades to come.

For Kristofferson himself, the Ryman show was a validation of the path he had chosen. The years of struggle, doubts, and criticism from those who said he was too old or too different for country music—all of it faded away in the face of the connection he had made with the audience. He had proven that authenticity and raw ability could transcend genre boundaries and speak directly to the hearts of listeners. In the days and weeks that followed, Kristofferson's fame grew meteorically. His albums flew off the shelves; his songs were covered by artists across the musical spectrum; and his presence was requested at every big music event. But for those who had been at the Ryman that night, Kristofferson would always be known as he was on that stage—a poet with a guitar, a man unafraid to lay bare his soul through his music. The Ryman concert became the stuff of legend, spoken about in reverential tones by music reviewers and fans alike. It marked the moment when

Kris Kristofferson

Kris Kristofferson truly found his voice and his audience, setting the stage for a career that would affect generations of songwriters and performers.

CHAPTER 1: MEET KRIS KRISTOFFERSON

Kristofferson was born on June 22, 1936, in Brownsville, Texas. From his earliest years, it was clear that Kristofferson was bound for an extraordinary life. The son of a U.S. Air Force major general, he grew up in a household that values discipline, education, and service to the country. This upbringing would shape his character and affect his diverse career path. As a child, Kristofferson moved frequently due to his father's military postings. This nomadic lifestyle exposed him to various cultures and experiences. Despite the constant moves, young Kris found stability in his love for literature and music. He began writing songs and short stories at an early age, showing a natural gift for storytelling that would become his hallmark. His academic prowess was obvious from the start. He excelled in school, finally earning a Rhodes Scholarship to Oxford University in England. At Oxford, he studied English literature, strengthening his love for words and their power. It was during this time that he also began to seriously explore his interest in music, playing in local pubs and honing his songwriting skills.

 After finishing his studies, Kristofferson joined the U.S. Army, following in his father's footsteps. He became a helicopter pilot and rose to the rank of captain. However, military life didn't quench his thirst for artistic expression. Throughout his service, he continued to write songs, dreaming of a future in music. In 1965, against his family's wishes, Kristofferson turned down an offer to teach English literature at West Point. Instead, he moved to Nashville to follow his true passion: songwriting. This decision marked the beginning of a challenging but ultimately rewarding journey in the music business. Kristofferson's early years in Nashville were far from flashy. He did odd jobs to make ends meet, including a stint as a janitor at Columbia Records. According to legend, he would occasionally land his chopper in Johnny Cash's yard to pitch him songs. This persistent and unconventional approach finally paid off. His success came when Roger Miller recorded "Me and

Bobby McGee" in 1969. The song became a hit, opening doors for Kristofferson in the music business. He quickly earned fame as a talented songwriter, penning hits for numerous artists, including Johnny Cash, Waylon Jennings, and Jerry Lee Lewis.

Kristofferson's own music career took off in the 1970s. His debut record, "Kristofferson," was released in 1970, showcasing his gravelly voice and poetic lyrics. His music defied straightforward categorization, blending aspects of country, folk, and rock. Songs like "Help Me Make It Through the Night," "For the Good Times," and "Sunday Mornin' Comin' Down" became classics, praised for their raw emotion and storytelling prowess. As his music career thrived, he also found success in Hollywood. He made his acting debut in "The Last Movie" (1971) and went on to star in numerous films, including "Alice Doesn't Live Here Anymore" (1974) and "A Star Is Born" (1976), alongside Barbra Streisand. His rugged attractive looks and natural charisma made him a famous leading man throughout the 1970s and 1980s. Throughout his life, Kristofferson has been known for his political activism and commitment to social issues. He has been an outspoken advocate for Native American rights, environmental problems, and veterans' causes. This activism has sometimes been controversial, but it has always been an important part of who he is as an artist and person.

 In his later years, he has faced health challenges, including a misdiagnosis of Alzheimer's disease that was later found to be Lyme disease. Despite these setbacks, he has continued to perform and create music, releasing albums and traveling well into his seventies. Kristofferson's hobbies and interests stretch beyond music and acting. He has a lifelong love of literature and poetry, frequently mentioning influences like William Blake and Walt Whitman in his work. He's also an avid sports fan, especially of boxing, and has been known to engage in friendly sparring matches. His work has been marked by numerous accolades. He was admitted into the Songwriters Hall of Fame in 1985 and the Country Music Hall of Fame in 2004. He has won multiple Grammy Awards and a Golden Globe for his performance. In 2014, he earned a lifetime achievement award from the Recording Academy. Kris Kristofferson's life story is one of amazing versatility and resilience. From Rhodes Scholar to Army captain, from janitor to music icon, he has lived many lives in one. His songs have touched millions, his films have entertained countless viewers, and his unwavering dedication to his beliefs has inspired many.

Early Life

The intersection of military discipline, intellectual curiosity, and a budding love for artistic expression shaped Kris Kristofferson's early life. Kristofferson entered the world as the first child of Mary Ann and Lars Henry Kristofferson. His father, a U.S. Army Air Corps soldier who later became a U.S. Air Force major general, instilled in young Kris a strong sense of duty and order from an early age. The Kristofferson family's military lifestyle meant frequent moves, a factor that would greatly influence Kris's worldview and later artistic perspective. As a child, he lived in different places across the United States, including Texas, California, and Illinois. This nomadic childhood exposed him to diverse cultures and experiences, sowing the seeds for his later ability to catch the essence of different American lifestyles in his songwriting.

Despite the constant relocations, his parents prioritized schooling and cultural enrichment. His mother, an avid reader with a degree in English literature, nurtured Kris's love for words and stories. From a young age, he was immersed in books, having a particular fondness for poetry and classic literature. This early exposure to the power of words would prove instrumental in shaping his future as a songwriter and performer. Kristofferson's childhood was marked by a blend of traditional values and intellectual interests. His family's strong Swedish-American heritage played a role in his upbringing, with a focus on hard work, perseverance, and academic success. At the same time, his artistic spark was starting to ignite. He started writing short stories and poems in grade school, showing a natural gift for crafting narratives and evoking emotions through words. Music also played a major role in Kristofferson's early life, though not initially in the form of songwriting. He learned to play the guitar as a teenager, but at this time, it was more of a hobby than a serious pursuit. His early musical influences were diverse, ranging from the country sounds he heard in Texas to the rock and roll that was starting to sweep the nation in the 1950s.

As a student, Kristofferson excelled intellectually. He was a standout in English and literature classes but also showed aptitude in sports, especially football and track. This mix of brains and brawn made him a well-rounded and popular student. His high school years in San Mateo, California, saw him emerge as a Golden Gloves boxer, showcasing the grit and drive that would serve him well in his later career. His childhood dreams were as varied as his abilities. At different points, he wanted to be a writer, following in the footsteps of his literary heroes. The military also held a strong appeal, influenced by his father's work and the sense of duty ingrained in him from an early age. There were times when he entertained the idea of becoming a professional athlete, driven by his success in sports. However, beneath these more conventional ambitions, a deeper, more artistic dream was taking root. Kristofferson was drawn to the idea of storytelling—capturing the human experience in words and music. While he may not have fully known it at the time, his childhood experiments with writing and music were laying the groundwork for his future career as a songwriter and performer.

 The tension between meeting family expectations and pursuing his own path became increasingly clear as Kristofferson approached adulthood. His father, thinking Kris would follow in his footsteps, encouraged a military career. His mother, recognizing his intellectual gifts, pushed for academic interests. Kristofferson, respectful of his parents' wishes but also feeling the pull of his own ambitions, tried to find a balance between these competing influences. His decision to take a Rhodes Scholarship to Oxford University was a turning point, one that satisfied his parents' hopes for his academic success while also opening new horizons for his personal and creative growth. Throughout his childhood and adolescence, Kristofferson was also developing the keen observational skills and empathy that would later guide his songwriting. Growing up in different parts of the country, he encountered people from all walks of life, absorbing their stories and experiences. This early exposure to the diversity of American life would prove invaluable in his later work, allowing him to write with authenticity about a wide range of human experiences.

As he entered adulthood, the seeds planted in his childhood—his love of books, his musical inclinations, his sense of duty, and his curiosity about the human condition—were ready to bloom. While his road to becoming a renowned songwriter and performer was not yet clear, the foundations were firmly in place. Kristofferson's early life was a time of formation, where the various strands of his personality and abilities were woven together. The discipline established by his military upbringing, the love of language nurtured by his mother, the diverse experiences gained from his nomadic childhood, and his own innate creativity all combined to shape the artist he would become. Whether he realized it or not, his early life was preparing him for a remarkable journey.

Love Life

Kris Kristofferson's love life has been as complicated and multifaceted as his career, marked by passionate relationships, marriages, and a large, blended family. His journey through love shows the same intensity and authenticity that characterize his music and acting. His first major romantic relationship began during his college years at Pomona College in California. He fell in love with his high school sweetheart, Fran Beer. Their relationship continued as Kristofferson sought his Rhodes Scholarship at Oxford University. In 1960, soon after returning from England and joining the U.S. Army, Kristofferson and Beer married. This union produced two children: a girl, Tracy, born in 1962, and a son, Kris, born in 1968. However, the demands of Kristofferson's burgeoning music business and the strains of his unconventional lifestyle began to take a toll on the marriage. As he spent more time in Nashville chasing his songwriting dreams, often living a hand-to-mouth existence, the relationship became strained. The couple divorced in 1969, just as Kristofferson's career was starting to take off.

The 1970s marked a time of both professional success and personal exploration for Kristofferson. As his star rose in the music and film industries, he became known for his rugged attractive looks and charismatic personality, traits that made him a sought-after partner in Hollywood circles. During this time, he had relationships with several high-profile women, including Janis Joplin and Barbra Streisand, though these were generally brief and often overlapped with professional collaborations. It was during this time that Kristofferson met singer Rita Coolidge. Their connection was immediate and intense, both emotionally and professionally. They began working musically, their voices and styles complementing each other beautifully. Kristofferson and Coolidge married in 1973, forming one of the music industry's most famous power couples of the 1970s. The Kristofferson-Coolidge partnership was fruitful both emotionally and professionally. They made several popular albums together and frequently toured as a duo. In 1974, they received a daughter, Casey. Their relationship seemed to embody the free-spirited ethos of the age, with both partners supporting each other's careers while building a family.

 However, the pressures of fame, combined with Kristofferson's struggles with alcohol and the demands of their jobs, began to strain the relationship. Despite their clear chemistry and shared successes, Kristofferson and Coolidge divorced in 1980. The split was painful for both, and its impact was obvious in their subsequent musical works. Following his divorce from Coolidge, Kristofferson entered a time of personal reevaluation. He focused on his career and co-parenting his children from previous marriages. It was during this time that he met Lisa Meyers, an attorney who would become his third and present wife. Kristofferson and Meyers married in 1983, marking the beginning of his longest and most stable love relationship. Together, they have five children: Jesse, Jody, Johnny, Kelly Marie, and Blake.

Kris Kristofferson

Their marriage has endured for nearly four decades, weathering the ups and downs of Kristofferson's work and personal challenges.

Lisa Meyers Kristofferson has been a steadfast partner, supporting Kris through different career transitions, health scares, and the natural aging process. She has also been instrumental in managing his business matters and helping to preserve his legacy. Their relationship is often cited as a stabilizing force in Kristofferson's life, giving him a strong family foundation as he navigated the later stages of his work. Kristofferson's approach to fatherhood has changed over the years. While his early work and lifestyle sometimes made consistent parenting challenging, he has made concerted efforts to be present in his children's lives. He has spoken openly about the regrets he has regarding his absence during his older children's early years and has tried to be a more involved father to his younger children. The blended Kristofferson family, consisting of eight children from three marriages, is a testament to Kris's capacity for love and his dedication to family. Despite the complexities inherent in such a large, blended family, Kristofferson has worked to keep relationships with all of his children and to build a sense of unity among his extended family.

Kristofferson's love life has not been without its controversies and difficulties. His high-profile relationships and marriages have often been subject to media scrutiny, and he has been open about his past problems with alcohol and the impact these had on his relationships. However, he has also been praised for his honesty in addressing these problems and for his efforts to grow and improve as a partner and father. Throughout his romantic journey, Kristofferson's experiences have often found their way into his songs. Many of his most poignant and famous songs deal with themes of love, loss, regret, and redemption, clearly drawing from his personal life. Songs like "For the Good Times" and "Help Me Make It Through the Night" resonate with listeners precisely because they capture the complex feelings of love and relationships that Kristofferson himself has experienced. As he has aged, Kristofferson's view on love has evolved. He has spoken about the depth and stability of his relationship with Lisa, crediting her with helping him find peace and meaning in his later years. This long-lasting marriage seems to have given him a sense of grounding that was perhaps missing in his earlier, more tumultuous relationships.

Kris Kristofferson's love life, much like his artistic career, has been a journey of growth, learning, and eventually, enduring commitment. From the youthful passion of his first marriage to the steady companionship of his current one, his experiences in love have shaped him as a person and as an artist, adding to the depth and authenticity that have made him an enduring figure in American culture.

CHAPTER 2: EDUCATIONAL JOURNEY

Kristofferson's educational journey is a testament to his intellectual prowess and the diverse inspirations that shaped his multifaceted career. From his early schooling to his prestigious academic successes, Kristofferson's path through education played a crucial role in forming the artist and writer he is. His high school years were spent at San Mateo High School in California, where the Kristofferson family had stayed for a time. It was here that Kris truly began to shine academically. He immersed himself in his studies, especially in English and literature classes, where his talent for writing and analysis became evident. His teachers noticed his exceptional ability to interpret complex texts and express his thoughts clearly and eloquently in writing. At San Mateo High, Kristofferson wasn't just known for his academic ability. He was also a standout athlete, playing in football and track. His participation in sports helped him develop discipline, teamwork skills, and physical toughness that would serve him well in his later military career and the often-grueling life of a touring musician. It was also during his high school years that Kristofferson took up fighting, becoming a Golden Gloves boxer. This combination of intellectual and physical activities helped shape his well-rounded personality.

Beyond academics and sports, Kristofferson's high school years saw the early flowering of his creative talents. He began writing poetry and short stories, often inspired by the works of classic authors he was learning in his English classes. While music wasn't yet a major focus, he did learn to play the guitar during this time, laying the foundation for his future songwriting career. His exceptional results in high school opened doors to prestigious universities. He decided to attend Pomona College in Claremont, California, beginning his studies there in 1954. At Pomona, Kristofferson's intellectual horizons grew dramatically. He majored in English Literature, diving deep into the works of Shakespeare, Chaucer, and other literary giants. His teachers were impressed by his keen analytical skills and his ability to draw insightful connections between texts. During his time at Pomona, Kristofferson continued to succeed both academically and in extracurricular activities. He was elected to Phi Beta Kappa, the oldest and most prestigious academic honor society in the United States, a recognition of his outstanding scholastic success. He also continued his athletic pursuits, playing rugby and keeping his interest in boxing.

It was at Pomona that Kristofferson's work began to take on a more serious tone. He contributed to the college's literary magazine and began to experiment with songwriting, though music was still secondary to his literary goals at this point. His time at Pomona also introduced him to a wide range of ideas and people, broadening his worldview and influencing his later socially conscious songwriting. His academic performance at Pomona was so impressive that he was given a prestigious Rhodes Scholarship to study at Oxford University in England. This was a major achievement, marking him as one of the top scholars in the country. In 1958, after graduating from Pomona,

Kristofferson crossed the Atlantic to begin his studies at Merton College, Oxford. At Oxford, Kristofferson's intellectual journey hit new heights. He pursued a Bachelor of Philosophy degree, focusing on English Literature with a particular emphasis on William Blake, the Romantic poet whose work would have a lasting impact on Kristofferson's own writing. The Oxford educational system, with its focus on independent study and critical thinking, suited Kristofferson's intellectual curiosity and self-directed learning style.

During his time at Oxford, Kristofferson's literary dreams flourished. He began work on a novel and continued to write poetry, honing his skill under the guidance of some of the world's most famous scholars. The rigorous academic environment pushed him to refine his analytical skills and expand his understanding of language and literature. However, Oxford wasn't all about academic interests for Kristofferson. It was here that his interest in music started to grow more serious. He started performing in local pubs, playing covers of famous folk and country songs as well as some of his own compositions. This experience gave him a taste of the performative side of music and helped him develop his stage presence. Kristofferson's time at Oxford also exposed him to a wide range of international views. He formed friendships with students from around the world, engaging in deep discussions about politics, philosophy, and society. These experiences would later inform his worldview and add to the social consciousness evident in much of his songwriting.

After finishing his studies at Oxford in 1960, Kristofferson faced a crossroads. Despite his obvious talent for academia and the possibility of an academic career, he felt pulled in other ways. His family, especially his father, hoped he would follow a military path. Kristofferson, respecting his family's wishes and feeling a sense of duty, chose to join the U.S. Army. While this choice marked the end of his formal academic journey, it didn't mean an end to his intellectual pursuits. During his military service, Kristofferson continued to read voraciously and write in his free time. He even taught English literature at the United States Military

Academy at West Point for a brief time, demonstrating that his academic background remained an integral part of his identity. His educational journey, from his high school days through his time at Oxford, played a key role in shaping the man he would become. The analytical skills he developed through his study of literature informed his approach to songwriting, allowing him to create lyrics that were both poetic and incisive. His exposure to classic literature and philosophy provided a wellspring of ideas and themes that he would draw upon throughout his artistic work. Moreover, the discipline and work ethic instilled by his rigorous academic interests served him well in the competitive worlds of music and film. The confidence he gained from his academic achievements gave him the courage to follow his artistic dreams, even when it meant defying expectations and taking significant risks.

Kristofferson's education also equipped him with a breadth of knowledge that set him apart in the entertainment business. His songs often incorporate literary allusions and complex themes, showing his deep engagement with literature and philosophy. This intellectual depth, paired with his everyman persona, made him a unique figure in popular music. The social awareness that became a hallmark of Kristofferson's work can also be traced back to his educational experiences. The exposure to diverse views and ideas during his time at Pomona and Oxford helped shape his progressive worldview. His songs often tackle social and political issues with a nuance and understanding that represent his broad education. While he finally chose a path that led him away from academia, the impact of his educational journey stayed evident throughout his career. In interviews, he often referenced literary works or philosophical concepts, showing how deeply ingrained his academic background was in his thinking. Kristofferson's journey through school is also a story of the transformative power of learning. From a military family background, his academic success opened up new worlds of possibility. They helped him to transcend the expectations set for him and forge his own unique path. This idea of personal transformation through knowledge and experience would become a recurring motif in his songwriting.

 In later years, Kristofferson's respect for education and intellectual pursuit stayed strong. He encouraged his own children to value learning and has been a supporter of different educational initiatives. His life story serves as an inspiration, showing that academic success and artistic creativity are not mutually exclusive, but can in fact enrich and inform each other. Kristofferson's educational journey, from San Mateo High School through Oxford University, laid the foundation for his remarkable success. It provided him with the tools to become not just a successful entertainer, but a thought-provoking artist whose work continues to resonate with depth and meaning. His story is a powerful reminder of the lasting effect that a rich and diverse education can have, even in fields far removed from the academic world.

CHAPTER 3: BEGINNING OF A SONGWRITING CAREER

Kristofferson's journey into songwriting is a tale of perseverance, ability, and a willingness to take risks. It's a story that starts long before his first hit song, rooted in his early love for literature and music, and shaped by his diverse life experiences. During his high school and college years, Kristofferson's main creative outlet was writing poetry and short stories. His talent for wordcraft, honed through his study of literature, would prove invaluable in his future songwriting efforts. Although he learned to play guitar as a teenager, at this point music was more of a hobby than a serious goal. It was during his time at Oxford University as a Rhodes Scholar that Kristofferson began to study songwriting more seriously. The vibrant folk music scene in England in the late 1950s and early 1960s introduced him to a new world of musical storytelling. He started performing in local pubs, mostly playing covers but rarely slipping in original compositions. These early performances were important in developing his confidence as a performer and helping him understand how to connect with an audience through music.

However, upon completing his studies at Oxford, Kristofferson's road seemed to lead away from music. He joined the U.S. Army, following in his father's path, and for several years, his creative pursuits took a back seat to his military duties. Yet, even during this time, he continued to write songs in his free moments, filling notebooks with lyrics and musical ideas. The real turning point came in 1965 when Kristofferson, despite family pressure and the promise of a stable military career, decided to follow his passion for music. He turned down an offer to teach English literature at West Point and instead moved to Nashville, the heart of the country music business. This choice marked the true beginning of his songwriting career, though success was far from immediate. His early days in Nashville were difficult. He did a variety of odd jobs to make ends meet, including as a janitor at Columbia Records. This position, while humble, proved fortuitous as it allowed him to be close to the music business and observe successful songwriters and performers up close.

 During this time, Kristofferson honed his craft relentlessly. He wrote constantly, drawing inspiration from his life experiences, the characters he met in Nashville, and the broader social and political climate of the 1960s. His military background, his academic schooling, and his newfound immersion in the world of country music all fed into his unique songwriting voice. His success as a songwriter came gradually. He began to make connections in the Nashville music scene, pitching his songs to known artists and producers. His determination paid off when Roger Miller recorded "Me and Bobby McGee" in 1969. This marked an important milestone in Kristofferson's career, providing him with his first major success as a songwriter. The success of "Me and Bobby McGee" opened doors for him. Other artists began to take notice of his ability, and soon his songs were being recorded by some of the biggest names in country and pop music. Johnny Cash, Waylon Jennings, and Jerry Lee Lewis were among the many singers who recorded Kristofferson's compositions. What set his songs apart was their poetic beauty and emotional depth. Drawing on his literary background, he created lyrics that were at once simple and profound. Songs like "Sunday Mornin' Comin' Down" and "Help Me Make It Through the Night" showcased his ability to capture complex human feelings in accessible, relatable terms.

 Kristofferson's songwriting style was also famous for its blending of genres. While rooted in country music traditions, his songs incorporated aspects of folk, rock, and even gospel. This cross-genre appeal allowed his music to reach a broad audience and added to his growing reputation as a songwriter. As his songs gained popularity, Kristofferson began to consider a future as a performer in his own right. In 1970, he released his self-titled debut record. While it wasn't an immediate commercial success, it established him as a unique voice in the music business. His gravelly voice and unpolished delivery may not have fit the traditional country music mold, but they gave an authenticity to his performances that resonated with listeners. The early 1970s saw

Kristofferson's songwriting career hit new heights. In 1971, Janis Joplin's posthumous release of "Me and Bobby McGee" became a number-one hit, exposing Kristofferson's writing to an even wider public. That same year, he won the Songwriter of the Year award at the Country Music Association Awards, a testament to his growing impact in the industry.

His success as a songwriter opened up possibilities in other areas of entertainment. He began to receive offers for acting parts, leading to a successful career in film alongside his music. This diversification of his career helped to further spread his reputation and offered new sources of inspiration for his songwriting. Throughout the 1970s, Kristofferson continued to write prolifically, both for himself and for other acts. His songs often touched on social and political issues, mirroring the turbulent times. One of the keys to his success as a songwriter was his ability to draw from his diverse life situations. His songs often featured characters and situations that represented the many worlds he had inhabited - from military life to academia, from the struggles of an aspiring artist to the complexities of fame. This breadth of experience gave a universality to his writing that appealed to a wide range of listeners. His approach to music was both disciplined and intuitive. He often spoke about the value of crafting and refining lyrics, drawing on his academic background in literature. At the same time, he stressed the need to remain open to moments of inspiration, often carrying a notebook to jot down ideas as they came to him.

As his career progressed, Kristofferson became known not just for his individual songs, but for his general body of work. His consistent output and the high quality of his writing established him as one of the most recognized songwriters of his age. He became a member of the Nashville Songwriters Hall of Fame in 1977, an acknowledgment of his important contributions to the craft. Throughout his career, Kristofferson stayed committed to pushing boundaries in his songwriting. He wasn't afraid to tackle controversial topics or to experiment with different musical styles. This willingness to take risks and grow as an artist helped to keep his writing fresh and relevant over the decades. His influence on the world of songwriting goes far beyond his own compositions. Many younger songwriters have mentioned him as an influence, admiring his poetic lyrics and his ability to tell compelling stories through song. His success helped to pave the way for other songwriters who didn't fit the standard country music mold, broadening the scope of what was possible within the genre.

CHAPTER 4: FIRST HIT

Kris Kristofferson's first hit as a songwriter came with the song "Me and Bobby McGee," a track that would become one of the most famous and enduring songs of the 20th century. The journey of this song from its creation to its final success is a story that encapsulates Kristofferson's struggle, talent, and the serendipitous nature of the music industry. The origin of "Me and Bobby McGee" can be traced back to 1969, during Kristofferson's early days in Nashville. At the time, he was working a number of jobs to make ends meet, including as a janitor at Columbia Records and a helicopter pilot for offshore oil rigs in the Gulf of Mexico. These experiences, particularly his time flying helicopters, would shape the vivid imagery and sense of wanderlust that permeate the song. He wrote "Me and Bobby McGee" at the advice of producer and Monument Records founder Fred Foster. Foster had stated to Kristofferson that he had a great idea for a song title - "Me and Bobby McKee." He was referring to Barbara

McKee, a secretary at Boudleaux Bryant's publishing company. Kristofferson misheard the name as "McGee," and the song began to take shape in his thoughts.

 The writing process for "Me and Bobby McGee" displayed his literary background and his ability to craft a compelling narrative within the framework of a song. He drew on the history of the American road story, creating a tale of two drifters traveling across the United States. The song's narrator and Bobby McGee hitchhike from Kentucky to California, feeling freedom and love along the way, only to part in the end. One of the most notable aspects of the song was his choice to leave Bobby McGee's gender ambiguous. This allowed listeners to interpret the connection in the song in different ways, adding to its universal appeal. It also mirrored Kristofferson's nuanced approach to music, avoiding simple categorizations and stereotypes. The song's structure and melody were relatively easy, but it was Kristofferson's lyrics that truly set it apart. Lines like "Freedom's just another word for nothin' left to lose" encapsulated complex ideas about freedom, loss, and the human condition in a way that resonated strongly with listeners. The song's blend of melancholy and optimism, combined with its vivid storytelling, would prove to be a winning combination. Once the song was completed, Kristofferson began to pitch it to different artists and producers in Nashville. Despite the quality of the writing, success didn't come quickly. The music business can be notoriously difficult to break into, and Kristofferson, despite his talent, was still an unknown quantity to many in Nashville.

 The first major recording of "Me and Bobby McGee" came in 1969 when Roger Miller cut the song. Miller's version hit number 12 on the Billboard country charts, providing Kristofferson with his first taste of success as a songwriter. This recording helped to bring attention to Kristofferson's work within the country music community, opening doors for further possibilities. However, it was Janis Joplin's recording of the song that eventually turned it into a massive hit and cemented Kristofferson's reputation as a songwriter of exceptional talent. Joplin recorded the song in October 1970, just days before her untimely death. Her version was released posthumously in 1971 as part of her album "Pearl." Joplin's raw, emotional delivery of the song, mixed with its release following her death, struck a chord with listeners. Her version of "Me and Bobby McGee" hit number one on the Billboard Hot 100 chart in March 1971, becoming Joplin's only number-one single and Kristofferson's first as a songwriter. The success of Joplin's recording pushed "Me and Bobby McGee" and Kristofferson himself into the national spotlight. The song's crossover appeal, resonating with both country and rock listeners, helped to establish Kristofferson as a songwriter capable of transcending genre borders.

For Kristofferson, the success of "Me and Bobby McGee" was life-changing. It provided him with financial stability for the first time since he had chosen to pursue a career in music. More importantly, it gave him credibility within the industry, making it easier for him to get his other songs recorded and opening up chances for him as a performer in his own right. The timing of the song's success overlapped with the release of Kristofferson's second album, "The Silver Tongued Devil and I," in 1971. The album included Kristofferson's own recording of "Me and Bobby McGee," allowing him to gain from the song's popularity as both a songwriter and a performer. This helped to start his career as a recording artist, a path that would run parallel to his continued success as a songwriter for other artists. In the years following its initial success, "Me and Bobby McGee" has been covered by numerous artists across various styles, testament to its enduring appeal and the strength of Kristofferson's writing. From country stars to rock bands, the song has proven its flexibility and timeless quality.

The success of "Me and Bobby McGee" also had a profound effect on Kristofferson's songwriting style. It reinforced his belief in the power of narrative songwriting and inspired him to continue exploring complex ideas within the framework of accessible, melodic songs. Many of his later hits, such as "Sunday Mornin' Comin' Down" and "Help Me Make It Through the Night," would follow a similar template of introspective lyrics paired with memorable melodies. Moreover, the song's success opened doors for him in other areas of culture. His newfound fame as a songwriter led to chances in acting, with Kristofferson making his film debut in "The Last Movie" in 1971. This marked the beginning of a successful parallel career in Hollywood that would cover several decades.

The journey of "Me and Bobby McGee" from its inception to its status as a classic hit encapsulates much of what makes Kristofferson's work so remarkable. It shows his ability to draw from his diverse life experiences to create universally relatable stories, his skill in crafting lyrics that are both poetic and accessible, and his knack for writing songs that resonate across genre boundaries. Ultimately, "Me and Bobby McGee" served as the launching pad for Kristofferson's long and varied career in music and movies. It established him as a major player in the songwriting world and set the stage for decades of creative output. The song's success story remains an inspiration to aspiring musicians, a reminder that with talent, determination, and a little bit of luck, a single song can change the trajectory of a career and leave an indelible mark on popular culture.

CHAPTER 5: THE HIGHWAYMEN

The Highwaymen, a country music supergroup formed in 1985, brought together four of the most iconic names in American music: Johnny Cash, Willie Nelson, Waylon Jennings, and Kris Kristofferson. This collaboration represented a pinnacle in country music history, uniting four artists who had each made important individual contributions to the genre and American popular culture. The genesis of The Highwaymen can be traced back to a chance meeting in Montreux, Switzerland, in 1984. Cash, Nelson, Jennings, and Kristofferson were all in the area for a live tribute to Carl Perkins. During their downtime, the four friends found themselves jamming together and reminiscing about their shared experiences in the music business. It was during these informal sessions that the idea of forming a supergroup started to take shape. The name "The Highwaymen" was inspired by the Jimmy Webb song "Highwayman," which would become the group's signature track and the title of their first album. The song's theme of reincarnation and its exploration of different characters throughout history resonated with the four artists, each of whom had lived eventful lives and carved out unique personas in the music world. What made The Highwaymen special was not just the star power of its members, but the genuine friendship and mutual respect that existed between them. Cash, Nelson, Jennings, and Kristofferson had known each other for years, having crossed paths numerous times throughout their lives. They had supported each other through personal and professional challenges, and their camaraderie was obvious in their performances and recordings.

The group's first record, "Highwayman," was released in 1985 to both critical acclaim and commercial success. The title track, featuring each member taking a verse as a different character, hit number one on the Billboard country music chart. This success showed that there was a strong appetite among fans for this collaboration of country music legends. The Highwaymen's music was defined by a blend of traditional country, outlaw country, and folk influences. Each member brought their unique style and voice to the project, producing a sound that was both familiar and fresh. Their harmonies, particularly on songs like "Desperados Waiting for a Train," showcased their ability to blend their unique sounds into a cohesive whole. Beyond their musical output, The Highwaymen marked a cultural phenomenon. They represented the spirit of the outlaw country movement, which had challenged the Nashville establishment in the 1970s with its raw, unvarnished approach to country music. By the 1980s, all four members of The Highwaymen were established icons, and their collaboration served as a celebration of their shared heritage.

The group's live shows were particularly memorable. Their concerts featured a mix of Highwaymen songs, solo hits from each member, and cover versions of famous country and folk tunes. These shows often had a loose, informal feel, with the four friends sharing stories and jokes between songs, giving audiences a glimpse into their genuine camaraderie. Following the success of their first album, The Highwaymen produced two more studio albums: "Highwayman 2" in 1990 and "The Road Goes on Forever" in 1995. While these albums may not have hit the commercial heights of their debut, they further cemented the group's legacy and provided fans with more chances to hear these four legends performing together. The Highwaymen also went on several tours throughout their active years. These shows were major events in the country music world, drawing large crowds eager to see four of the genre's biggest stars on one stage. The concerts often had a retrospective feel, celebrating not just The Highwaymen's work together, but the individual lives of each member.

One of the most important aspects of The Highwaymen was how it impacted the later careers of its members. For Cash and Jennings in particular, who had seen their commercial fortunes wane somewhat in the 1980s, The Highwaymen offered a resurgence of popularity and a reminder of their enduring impact on country music. For Nelson and Kristofferson, who were still enjoying major success in their solo careers, The Highwaymen offered a chance to collaborate with old friends and reach new audiences. The group also played a part in introducing these legendary artists to younger generations. Many younger fans who might not have been familiar with the individual work of Cash, Nelson, Jennings, or Kristofferson were drawn to The Highwaymen's music, leading them to study the rich back catalogs of each artist. Despite their success and the joy they found in working together, The Highwaymen faced difficulties. Coordinating the schedules of four busy, in-demand artists was often tough. Each member continued to pursue solo projects and other collaborations, which sometimes limited the time they could give to The Highwaymen. Additionally, as the years went on, health issues began to affect some members of the group, especially Jennings and Cash.

The Highwaymen's busy years as a recording and touring entity came to an end in 1995, following the release of their third album. However, the members continued to appear together occasionally at special events and on each other's recordings. The bond between them stayed strong, even as their formal collaboration wound down. Their legacy goes far beyond their recorded output. They represented a unique moment in music history, a coming together of four artists who had each played a key role in shaping country music and American popular culture. Their collaboration celebrated their shared past and the enduring power of their music. In the years since The Highwaymen's active time, the group has been the subject of numerous documentaries, books, and tribute concerts. Their influence can be seen in later country music supergroups and in the continuing tradition of collaboration in country music. The passing of Jennings in 2002 and Cash in 2003 marked the end of an era, making it impossible for The Highwaymen to ever rejoin in their original form. However, Nelson and Kristofferson have continued to honor the legacy of the group, often playing Highwaymen songs in their solo shows and speaking fondly of their time with the supergroup. In the annals of country music history, they hold a special place. They were more than just a supergroup; they were a celebration of friendship, musical tradition, and the enduring spirit of country music. Their legacy continues to inspire artists and fans alike, ensuring that the music and the memory of The Highwaymen will indeed go on forever.

CHAPTER 6: ACTING DEBUT

Kris Kristofferson's acting debut marked a major expansion of his already impressive career in the entertainment industry. Known primarily as a songwriter and musician, Kristofferson's transition to acting in the early 1970s showed his versatility as an artist and opened up new avenues for his creative expression. His entry into the world of acting came at a time when his music career was hitting new heights. His songs were being recorded by major artists, and he was getting recognition as a performer in his own right. This success in the music industry, combined with his rugged, appealing looks and natural charisma, made him an attractive prospect for Hollywood producers looking for fresh talent. In "The Last Movie," Kristofferson played the part of Marin, a wrangler working on a Western film being shot in Peru. While his part was not the lead, it provided Kristofferson with valuable on-screen experience and exposed him to the filmmaking process. The film's unconventional narrative structure and

Hopper's unorthodox directing style made it a challenging project for a first-time actor, but Kristofferson approached the part with the same dedication he brought to his music.

Although "The Last Movie" was not a commercial success and got mixed reviews, Kristofferson's performance was noted by many critics. His natural presence on screen and his ability to communicate complex emotions without overacting caught the attention of other filmmakers. This initial step into acting, despite the film's limited success, opened doors for Kristofferson in Hollywood. Following his debut, Kristofferson's acting career quickly gained steam. His next major role came in 1972 in the film "Cisco Pike," where he played the titular character, a musician and drug dealer trying to go straight. This role allowed Kristofferson to draw on his own experiences in the music business, lending authenticity to his portrayal. The film, while not a blockbuster, further demonstrated Kristofferson's potential as an actor and his ability to carry a lead role. 1973 saw Kristofferson take on two important roles that would help establish him as a serious actor. In "Pat Garrett and Billy the Kid," directed by Sam Peckinpah, Kristofferson played the part of Billy the Kid opposite James Coburn's Pat Garrett. This Western gave him the chance to work with a famous director and a cast of experienced actors, further honing his craft. His portrayal of the famous outlaw was praised for its depth and nuance, showing that Kristofferson could hold his own alongside Hollywood veterans.

 The same year, Kristofferson played in "Blume in Love," a romantic comedy-drama directed by Paul Mazursky. This film showcased Kristofferson's versatility, showing that he could handle lighter, more comedic roles as well as dramatic ones. His performance in "Blume in Love" helped to broaden perceptions of him as an actor, showing that he wasn't limited to playing variations of his musical persona. Kristofferson's early acting career hit a high point in 1976 with his role in "A Star Is Born" opposite Barbra Streisand. This remake of the classic Hollywood story allowed Kristofferson to combine his musical abilities with his growing acting skills. Playing John Norman Howard, a rock star on the decline who helps launch the career of a young singer, Kristofferson delivered a powerful performance that resonated with audiences and reviewers alike. The film was a big commercial success and earned Kristofferson a Golden Globe for Best Actor in a Motion Picture—Musical or Comedy. Throughout his early acting career, he managed to balance his film work with his music. This dual career path allowed him to bring authenticity to roles that involved music while also giving him the chance to explore characters far removed from his public image as a singer-songwriter. His ability to move between these two worlds added to his unique appeal as an actor.

 One of Kristofferson's challenges in his transition to acting was overcoming preconceptions based on his history and music career. Some critics and audiences initially saw him as a musician trying his hand at acting rather than a serious actor in his own right. However, through his choice of diverse and challenging roles, he gradually earned respect for his acting skills, separate from his musical fame. His approach to acting was defined by a naturalistic style that drew on his own life experiences. He often spoke about the parallels between songwriting and acting, noting that both needed emotional honesty and the ability to convey complex feelings in a relatable way. This approach served him well, especially in parts that called for a rugged, world-weary character not dissimilar from the persona he had cultivated in his music. As he got more experience in film, Kristofferson began to take on a wider variety of roles. He appeared in action films, dramas, and even science fiction movies, showing his range as an actor. While not every film was a critical or commercial success, his performances were constantly praised for their sincerity and depth.

Kristofferson's acting career also benefited from his partnerships with respected directors. In addition to working with Dennis Hopper and Sam Peckinpah early in his career, he went on to work with directors like Martin Scorsese, John Sayles, and Alan Rudolph. These collaborations not only provided Kristofferson with opportunities to grow as an actor, but also gave credibility to his status as a serious performer in the film industry. The impact of Kristofferson's acting debut and subsequent career went beyond his own personal success. He was part of a wave of musicians who successfully moved into acting during the 1970s, helping to break down barriers between different areas of entertainment. His success opened the way for other musicians to explore acting opportunities, adding to a more fluid relationship between the music and film industries. His acting work also influenced his music. The storytelling skills he acquired as an actor influenced his songwriting, adding new depth and narrative complexity to his lyrics. Conversely, his musical background brought a unique rhythm and cadence to his line delivery as an actor, adding to his distinctive on-screen presence.

As Kristofferson's acting career progressed, he began to take on parts in television as well as film. This expansion into TV allowed him to reach new groups and explore long-form storytelling. His appearances in TV movies and miniseries further demonstrated his versatility as an actor, and they helped to keep him in the public eye even when he wasn't releasing new music or acting in major films. Looking back on Kristofferson's acting debut and early career, it's clear that his transition into film was more than just a side project or a short diversion from his music career. Instead, it represented a major artistic evolution, allowing him to express himself in new ways and reach new audiences. His success in both music and film cemented his status as a multi-talented artist and added to his enduring legacy in American popular culture. His journey from songwriter to actor is a testament to his artistic versatility and his desire to take risks. His acting debut opened up new creative avenues for him, allowing him to tell stories and explore characters in ways that complemented and built upon his work in music. The effect of this career expansion continues to be felt, both in Kristofferson's own body of work and in the broader landscape of entertainment, where the lines between different forms of artistic expression have become increasingly blurred.

CHAPTER 7: BREAKTHROUGH ROLE

Kristofferson's breakthrough role in cinema came with the 1976 film "A Star Is Born," a remake of the classic Hollywood tale that had already seen two successful iterations in 1937 and 1954. This version, directed by Frank Pierson and co-starring Barbra Streisand, offered the perfect vehicle for Kristofferson to showcase both his acting prowess and his musical talents, solidifying his position as a bona fide movie star. In the film, he portrays John Norman Howard, a rock star grappling with the waning days of his career and battling alcoholism and disillusionment with the music business. His character meets and falls in love with Esther Hoffman, played by Streisand, a talented but undiscovered singer whom he helps launch to fame. As Esther's career ascends, John's continues to fall, creating a poignant narrative about fame, love, and sacrifice. The role of John Norman Howard was tailored to Kristofferson's skills and public persona. It allowed him to draw upon his experiences in the music business, infusing the character with an authenticity that resonated with viewers. The world-weary, troubled rock star was not far away from the outlaw country image Kristofferson had cultivated in his music career, making his portrayal all the more convincing.

What set this performance apart from his earlier acting work was the depth and humanity Kristofferson brought to the role. While his previous films had showcased his rugged charm and natural screen presence, "A Star Is Born" needed him to delve into more complex emotional territory. The character's struggles with addiction, his feelings of inadequacy in the face of his partner's rising fame, and his ultimate act of self-sacrifice required a level of nuanced performance that Kristofferson delivered with remarkable skill. The on-screen chemistry between Kristofferson and Streisand was palpable, contributing greatly to the film's success. Their scenes together crackled with tension, tenderness, and passion, making the love story at the heart of the film incredibly compelling. This chemistry was particularly obvious in the musical performances, where their voices and stage presence complemented each other beautifully. Speaking of music, "A Star Is Born" provided him with the perfect chance to merge his two careers. The film's soundtrack, featuring songs performed by both Kristofferson and Streisand, was a huge commercial success. It allowed Kristofferson to showcase his musical skills to a wider audience, many of whom may have been more familiar with his acting work than his music at that point.

 The film's production was not without its difficulties. Reports of tension between Streisand and Kristofferson circulated, with some saying that Streisand, also serving as a producer on the film, was overshadowing her co-star. However, whatever off-screen difficulties may have existed, they did not detract from the final result. If anything, the stated tension may have added to the on-screen dynamic between their characters. Upon its release, "A Star Is Born" was a commercial and critical hit. It earned over $80 million at the box office, making it one of the highest-grossing films of 1976. Critics praised the performances of both stars, with many singling out Kristofferson for his raw and honest portrayal of John Norman Howard. The film's success turned into accolades for Kristofferson. He won the Golden Globe for Best Actor in a Motion Picture—Musical or Comedy—a major achievement that validated his status as a serious actor. This award, coming just a few years after his acting debut, showed how quickly he had developed his craft and gained recognition in the film industry.

The effect of "A Star Is Born" on Kristofferson's career cannot be overstated. It catapulted him from a respected character actor to a leading man capable of carrying out a big Hollywood production. The film's success opened doors to a wider range of roles and increased his business cachet. Directors and producers who might have been hesitant to cast a singer-turned-actor in leading roles now saw him as a bankable star. Moreover, the role allowed him to break free from the typecasting that had come to define his early acting career. While he had often been cast as rugged, taciturn characters in Westerns or action pictures, John Norman Howard was a more complex and emotionally vulnerable character. This performance showcased Kristofferson's acting range and paved the way for more diverse roles in the future. The success of "A Star Is Born" also had a significant effect on Kristofferson's music career. The film and its soundtrack exposed his music to a wider audience, many of whom may not have been familiar with his work as a songwriter and performer. This crossover success helped to revitalize his music career, which had started to plateau in the mid-1970s.

In the years following "A Star Is Born," Kristofferson's acting career continued to grow. He took on a range of roles in films such as "Semi-Tough" (1977), "Heaven's Gate" (1980), and "Songwriter" (1984), further showcasing his versatility as an actor. While none of these films hit the commercial heights of "A Star Is Born," they helped to establish him as a reliable and talented leading man in Hollywood. The breakthrough role also had a lasting effect on Kristofferson's approach to acting. The experience of playing John Norman Howard, a character with significant depth and emotional complexity, seemed to influence his choices in future roles. He increasingly gravitated towards characters with internal struggles and moral ambiguities, bringing the same level of nuanced performance to these roles that he had displayed in "A Star Is Born." It's worth noting that the success of this breakthrough came at a time when the lines between the music and film industries were becoming increasingly blurred. Kristofferson was at the forefront of this trend, along with peers like David Bowie and Mick Jagger, who were also making forays into acting. His success helped to pave the way for future musicians who would try their hand at acting, showing that it was possible to excel in both fields.

The impact of Kristofferson's performance in "A Star Is Born" continues to resonate in popular culture. The film has become a classic, usually cited as one of the best musical dramas of the 1970s. His portrayal of John Norman Howard is often held up as a great example of a musician successfully transitioning to acting, keeping authenticity while also showcasing genuine acting talent.

Kris Kristofferson

In retrospect, "A Star Is Born" marked the perfect confluence of factors for Kristofferson's breakthrough part. It allowed him to draw on his musical background, tap into his natural charisma, and stretch his acting skills all at once. The film's themes of fame, artistic integrity, and personal sacrifice resonated with his own experiences in the music business, lending an extra layer of authenticity to his performance. The role also came at the right time in Kristofferson's career. He had already established himself as a credible actor through his earlier films, but had yet to find that one defining part that would cement his place as a leading man. John Norman Howard provided that chance, allowing Kristofferson to showcase the full range of his talents to a global audience. Ultimately, Kristofferson's breakthrough role in "A Star Is Born" is a testament to his versatility as an artist and his willingness to take on difficult, complex characters. It marked the beginning of a new chapter in his career, one that would see him continue to balance his musical and acting interests with remarkable success. The effect of this performance continues to be felt, both in Kristofferson's enduring legacy and in the broader landscape of entertainment, where the barriers between different forms of artistic expression have become increasingly permeable.

CHAPTER 8: "THE SILVER TONGUED DEVIL AND I"

"The Silver Tongued Devil and I" is Kris Kristofferson's second studio album, released in 1971. This album played a crucial part in establishing Kristofferson as a formidable recording artist in his own right, building on the foundation laid by his self-titled debut album the previous year. It marked a major step forward in his career, showcasing his growth as a songwriter and performer. The album's title track, "The Silver Tongued Devil and I," sets the tone for the entire record. It's a self-reflective piece that addresses themes of charm, deception, and self-awareness. The song's protagonist admits his own tendency to use his charisma and way with words to manipulate situations and people. This introspective method is characteristic of Kristofferson's songwriting, blending personal events with broader observations about human nature. Musically, the album shows a refinement of his sound. While his debut album had a somewhat raw, unpolished feel, "The Silver

Tongued Devil and I" shows a more polished production approach. The arrangements are more complex, combining a wider range of instruments and studio techniques. However, the record still maintains the gritty, authentic feel that had become Kristofferson's trademark.

One of the standout tracks on the record is "Loving Her Was Easier (than Anything I'll Ever Do Again)." This song became one of Kristofferson's most beloved compositions, covered by numerous artists over the years. Its poetic lyrics and memorable melody exemplify Kristofferson's ability to make songs that are both deeply personal and widely relatable. The song's success helped to further cement his reputation as one of the premier songwriters of his time. Another notable track is "The Pilgrim, Chapter 33," which works as a kind of musical self-portrait. In this song, Kristofferson reflects on his journey as an artist and the different experiences that have shaped him. He references friends and fellow musicians, providing a vivid picture of the countercultural music scene of the late 1960s and early 1970s. This song, in particular, shows Kristofferson's skill at blending the personal with the universal, turning his own experiences into a broader commentary on the artist's life. The record also includes "Jody and the Kid," a poignant story-song about a May-December romance. This track demonstrates Kristofferson's ability to build fully-realized characters and narratives within the confines of a single song. It's a wonderful example of his talent for storytelling through music, a skill that would serve him well in his later career as an actor.

"The Silver Tongued Devil and I" was released at a time when Kristofferson's star was fast rising. His songs were being recorded by major artists, and he was getting recognition as a performer in his own right. This album played a major role in solidifying his standing as more than just a songwriter for other artists, but as a compelling recording artist himself. The album's commercial performance showed his growing popularity. It hit number 21 on the Billboard 200 chart and spawned several successful singles. This commercial success, coupled with critical acclaim, helped to expand Kristofferson's audience beyond the country music world and into the larger realm of popular music. Lyrically, the album showcases Kristofferson's poetic sensibilities and his ability to handle complex topics. Many of the songs deal with problems of identity, morality, and the human condition. Kristofferson's background in literature (he was a Rhodes Scholar who studied English literature at Oxford) is obvious in his sophisticated use of language and metaphor. The production of the album, handled by Fred Foster, strikes a balance between highlighting Kristofferson's raw, emotive vocals and creating a fuller, more layered sound than his debut. The use of strings, backing vocals, and a variety of instruments adds depth to the arrangements without overshadowing Kristofferson's performance or the purity of the songs.

"The Silver Tongued Devil and I" also shows the changing landscape of country music in the early 1970s. Kristofferson, along with artists like Willie Nelson and Waylon Jennings, was at the forefront of the outlaw country movement, which tried to break away from the polished, commercial sound that dominated Nashville at the time. This record, with its blend of country, folk, and rock influences, exemplifies the more individualistic, authentic approach that characterized outlaw country. "The Silver Tongued Devil and I" had an impact beyond its initial release. Many of the songs on the album became staples of Kristofferson's live performances and have been covered by various artists over the years. The album helped to establish Kristofferson's unique voice in the music world—a voice that combined poetic lyrics, a distinctive vocal style, and a willingness to handle complex topics. This album marks a crucial stepping stone in his career. It built on the promise of his debut, expanding his musical palette and demonstrating his artistic growth. The success of "The Silver Tongued Devil and I" paved the way for his future musical endeavors and added to his growing profile in the entertainment industry, which would soon lead to opportunities in film. Moreover, the album captures Kristofferson at a pivotal moment in his life and work. Having already achieved success as a songwriter, he was now establishing himself as a recording artist and on the cusp of starting his acting career. The songs on "The Silver Tongued Devil and I" reflect this time of transition, filled with self-reflection, observations about fame and identity, and meditations on love and loss.

In retrospect, "The Silver-Tongued Devil and I" stands as one of Kristofferson's defining works. It encapsulates his skills as a singer and performer, showcasing his poetic lyrics, his gravelly, emotive vocals, and his ability to blend elements of country, folk, and rock into a cohesive, distinctive sound. The record continues to be celebrated by fans and critics alike, a testament to its enduring quality and Kristofferson's artistry. Many artists in the Americana and alt-country genres, in particular, can draw a line of influence back to this album and Kristofferson's work in general. It expanded his audience, and showcased the full range of his talents as a songwriter and performer. The album remains a powerful testament to his artistry and his major contribution to American popular music.

CHAPTER 9: CHALLENGES AND TRIUMPHS

Kris Kristofferson's career has been marked by a series of challenges and successes that have shaped him into the iconic figure he is today. From his early struggles as an aspiring songwriter to his later fights with health issues, Kristofferson's journey is a testament to his resilience and dedication to his craft. One of the first major challenges Kristofferson faced was his choice to pursue a career in music against his family's wishes. After completing his Rhodes Scholarship at Oxford and serving in the military, he made the bold choice to turn down a teaching post at West Point to chase his dream of becoming a songwriter in Nashville. This decision led to a period of significant hardship, as he worked odd jobs, including as a janitor at Columbia Records, to make ends meet while trying to break into the music business. During this early phase of his work, he faced numerous rejections and setbacks. Many in Nashville were skeptical of his unconventional background and poetic writing style, which didn't fit nicely into the established country music formula. However, his persistence paid off when Roger Miller recorded "Me and Bobby McGee" in 1969, giving Kristofferson his first big success as a songwriter.

This triumph opened doors for Kristofferson, leading to more of his songs being recorded by famous artists. However, he faced a new challenge as he moved from being a songwriter to a performer in his own right. His gravelly voice and unpolished stage appearance were initially met with mixed reactions, and he had to work hard to establish himself as a credible recording artist. His venture into acting offered another set of challenges. Despite his natural charisma, he had to prove himself in a new area where his musical fame didn't necessarily translate. He suffered abuse from those who saw him as just another musician trying his hand at acting. However, through dedication and a willingness to take on diverse parts, he gradually gained respect in the film industry, culminating in his breakthrough performance in "A Star Is Born" in 1976. He has faced personal challenges throughout his career. His struggles with alcohol addiction in the 1970s threatened both his personal life and his work success. However, he managed to overcome this hurdle, eventually achieving sobriety and using his experiences to inform his art and his advocacy work.

Kristofferson faced one of his most significant challenges when he started experiencing memory problems. Initially misdiagnosed with Alzheimer's disease, he continued to act and create despite the uncertainty and fear surrounding his condition. This time was particularly trying, as he struggled with the possibility of losing his ability to write and perform. However, in a major triumph, it was later found that Kristofferson's cognitive problems were actually due to Lyme disease, which is treatable. This diagnosis led to a remarkable recovery, allowing him to continue his work and regain much of his lost cognitive function. This experience not only showed Kristofferson's resilience but also raised awareness about the importance of accurate medical diagnoses. He has also faced political activism challenges throughout his career. His outspoken stance on various social and political issues, including his criticism of U.S. foreign policy and his support for Native American rights, has sometimes put him at odds with more conservative elements of the country music audience. However, he has stayed true to his convictions, using his platform to speak out on issues he believes in, even when it might have been easier or more commercially advantageous to stay silent.

One of Kristofferson's most important triumphs has been his ability to maintain a relevant and respected career across multiple decades and artistic disciplines. From his early success as a songwriter in the 1970s to his acclaimed acting parts in the 1990s, and his continued musical output into the 21st century, he has shown a remarkable ability to evolve and adapt while staying true to his artistic vision. His induction into the Country Music Hall of Fame in 2004 and the Songwriters Hall of Fame in 1985 stand as recognition of his enduring effect on American music. These honors, along with his Grammy Lifetime Achievement Award in

2014, serve as a testament to the respect he has earned from his peers and the business as a whole. Another triumph has been Kristofferson's impact on subsequent generations of artists. Many singer-songwriters mention him as an inspiration, both for his poetic lyrics and his willingness to tackle complex topics in his music. His success in blending elements of country, folk, and rock helped pave the way for the Americana genre and affected the direction of country music as a whole.

Kristofferson's ability to balance his various artistic interests—music, acting, and writing—is another notable triumph. Few artists have achieved the level of success he has in multiple fields, and his ability to move between these different forms of expression has allowed him to reach a wide and varied audience. In his personal life, Kristofferson's long-lasting marriage to his third wife, Lisa, and his relationship with his eight children from his different marriages, can be seen as a triumph over the personal turmoil he experienced earlier in his life. His ability to keep these relationships while managing a demanding career demonstrates a level of personal growth and commitment. Despite having numerous challenges, including health scares, addiction, and business skepticism, Kristofferson has emerged as one of the most respected figures in American entertainment. His journey serves as an inspiration, showing that with talent, perseverance, and a willingness to evolve, it's possible to overcome significant hurdles and leave a lasting effect on popular culture. As he enters his later years, Kristofferson continues to perform and create, meeting the challenges of aging with the same grace and determination that have characterized his entire career. His ongoing artistic output and continued impact on new generations of artists stand as a testament to his enduring relevance and timeless quality of work.

CHAPTER 10 : AWARDS AND RECOGNITIONS

Kris Kristofferson, the legendary American singer-songwriter, actor, and musician, has earned numerous awards and recognitions throughout his illustrious career spanning over five decades. His contributions to music, film, and popular culture have been widely recognized by various organizations and institutions, cementing his position as a true icon in the entertainment industry. In the world of music, Kristofferson's accolades are particularly impressive. One of his most important achievements came in 1970, when he was awarded the prestigious Songwriter of the Year award at the Country Music Association Awards. This recognition was a testament to his exceptional songwriting skills and the effect his compositions had on the country music scene. The same year, he also received the Song of the Year award for "Sunday Mornin' Comin' Down," a poignant and introspective piece that showed his ability to write deeply moving lyrics.

Kristofferson's songwriting prowess continued to gain recognition throughout the 1970s. In 1971, he won the Grammy Award for Best Country Song for "Help Me Make It Through the Night," an emotional ballad that became one of his signature tunes. This victory not only highlighted his skill as a songwriter, but also demonstrated his ability to create songs that resonated with both critics and audiences. The Academy of Country Music also honored Kristofferson's services to the genre. In 1970, he won the ACM Song of the Year award for "Sunday Mornin' Comin' Down," further solidifying his reputation as one of country music's most gifted songwriters. This recognition from his peers in the country music business was a clear indication of the respect and admiration he had earned within the community. As his work progressed, he continued to earn accolades for his musical achievements. In 1973, he was inducted into the Nashville Songwriters Hall of Fame, an honor that recognized his significant effect on the art of songwriting and his lasting influence on the country music genre. This induction made him one of the most revered songwriters in the history of country music, acknowledging his role in shaping the genre's sound and storytelling traditions.

His impact extended beyond the country music scene, and his contributions to popular music as a whole were recognized in 2004 when he was inducted into the Country Music Hall of Fame. This prestigious award commemorated his lasting impact on the genre and his role in bridging the gap between country music and other popular styles. The induction event featured Kristofferson's unique ability to mix poetic lyrics with memorable melodies, creating songs that have become timeless classics. In addition to his musical accomplishments, Kristofferson's work in film has also been honored with several awards and nominations. His acting career, which began in the early 1970s, brought him critical praise and further expanded his artistic repertoire. In 1976, he earned a Golden Globe nomination for Best Actor in a Motion Picture—Musical or Comedy for his role in "A Star Is Born," opposite Barbra Streisand. This nomination demonstrated his versatility as a performer, as well as his ability to captivate audiences on the big screen and through his music. The recognition of Kristofferson's diverse skills continued throughout his career. In 1985, he was inducted into the Songwriters Hall of Fame, an award that celebrated his enduring effect on popular music across multiple genres. This induction acknowledged his ability to craft songs that transcended musical boundaries and spoke to the human experience in profound and universal ways.

Kristofferson's impact on American culture and his contributions to the arts were further recognized in 2009 when he received the BMI Icon Award. This prestigious award, given by Broadcast Music, Inc., celebrated his long-standing career and his status as a true legend in the music industry. The award recognized not only his success as a songwriter and performer, but also his role in inspiring and influencing generations of artists across various genres. In 2014, his lifetime of successes was honored with the Grammy Lifetime Achievement Award. This special merit award acknowledged his exceptional contributions to the recording industry and his enduring impact on music. His influence on literature and poetry has also been acknowledged. In 2012, he was given the PEN New England's Song Lyrics of Literary Excellence Award, recognizing the poetic quality of his lyrics and their literary merit. This award highlighted the depth and artistry of Kristofferson's songwriting, putting him in the company of other famous lyricists who have elevated songwriting to a form of literature.

 The film industry continued to recognize Kristofferson's accomplishments throughout his career. In 2013, he was named the American Veteran Awards Veteran of the Year, recognizing not only his artistic achievements but also his military service and advocacy for veterans' rights. This award demonstrated the multifaceted nature of Kristofferson's effect on American society, encompassing his artistic endeavors as well as his personal commitments and ideals. His impact on country music and his role in bridging different musical styles were further celebrated in 2017 when he received the Willie Nelson Lifetime Achievement Award at the Country Music Association Awards. This honor recognized his enduring effect on the genre and his status as a trailblazer who helped shape the direction of country music. He has also earned numerous other recognitions throughout his career. He has received multiple BMI Country Awards for his songwriting, acknowledging the economic success and cultural impact of his compositions. His songs have also won him several ASCAP Country Music Awards, further testament to their enduring popularity and influence.

Kristofferson's contributions to film have been recognized by different film festivals and organizations. He has received lifetime achievement awards from several international film festivals, celebrating his body of work as an actor and his effect on cinema. These awards have recognized his ability to bring depth and authenticity to his roles, as well as his status as a cultural icon whose presence on screen carries significant weight. The music business has continued to celebrate Kristofferson's legacy in recent years. He has been honored with tribute concerts and special performances at major award shows, with current artists paying homage to his influential catalog of songs. These tributes have not only celebrated his past successes but have also introduced his music to new generations of listeners, ensuring that his artistic legacy continues to grow. His influence on American culture has been recognized beyond the realms of music and film. He has earned honorary degrees from several universities, acknowledging his contributions to the arts and his role as a cultural figure. These academic awards have honored not only his artistic achievements, but also his intellectual contributions and ability to articulate complex ideas through his art.

In the realm of social activism, Kristofferson's efforts have also been honored. He has received awards from various organizations for his advocacy work, especially in areas related to social justice, environmental causes, and veterans' rights. These awards have recognized his use of his platform to raise awareness about important issues and his commitment to making a positive impact on society. Kristofferson's impact on the craft of songwriting has been celebrated through different workshops and educational programs. He has been invited to talk at songwriting seminars and has earned recognition for his role in mentoring young songwriters. These acknowledgements have highlighted his ongoing influence on the art of songwriting and his willingness to share his knowledge and experience with emerging artists. The depth and breadth of his career have also been recognized through different lifetime achievement awards from music business organizations, film societies, and cultural institutions. These awards have celebrated the totality of his contributions to American culture, recognizing his role as a songwriter, performer, actor, and cultural icon. These awards not only reflect his artistic achievements, but also acknowledge his role in shaping American popular culture and his ongoing legacy as one of the most influential figures in entertainment history.

CHAPTER 11:

COLLABORATION WITH

OTHER STARS

Kris Kristofferson's career has been marked by numerous collaborations with other stars across various forms of music and entertainment. These relationships have not only enriched his artistic output but have also helped to cement his status as a versatile and important figure in the worlds of music and film. One of Kristofferson's most famous collaborations was with country music legend Johnny Cash. Their friendship and musical partnership spanned decades, beginning in the late 1960s when Cash recorded Kristofferson's song "Sunday Mornin' Comin' Down." This collaboration proved to be a turning point in Kristofferson's career, helping to establish him as a songwriter of exceptional skill. Cash and Kristofferson went on to work together on numerous occasions, including live shows and recordings. They were both part of the country supergroup The

Highwaymen, along with Willie Nelson and Waylon Jennings, which further solidified their musical bond.

The Highwaymen, formed in 1985, marked one of the most significant collaborations in country music history. This supergroup brought together four of the genre's most respected artists, each with their own unique style and fanbase. Kristofferson's involvement in The Highwaymen allowed him to showcase his skills alongside some of country music's greatest legends. The group released three studio albums and went on several successful tours, with their performances becoming highly anticipated events in the country music world. Kristofferson's gifts to The Highwaymen included his songwriting skills, his distinctive vocal style, and his ability to blend seamlessly with the other members of the group. Another important collaboration in Kristofferson's career was with Barbra Streisand in the 1976 film "A Star Is Born." This project saw Kristofferson not only acting opposite Streisand but also adding to the film's music. The movie's theme song, "Evergreen," co-written by Streisand and Paul Williams, won an Academy Award for Best Original Song. His performance in the film, both as an actor and a singer, helped to broaden his appeal beyond the country music audience and established him as a credible leading man in Hollywood.

His collaborative spirit expanded to his work with fellow singer-songwriter and actress Rita Coolidge. The two were married from 1973 to 1980, and during this time, they made several duet albums that showcased their musical chemistry. Their 1973 album "Full Moon" was particularly successful, featuring the hit single "A Song I'd Like to Sing." Kristofferson and Coolidge's collaborations blended country, rock, and pop elements, appealing to a wide range of listeners and further demonstrating Kristofferson's versatility as an artist. Throughout his career, Kristofferson has worked with numerous other country music stars. He has written songs for and played with artists such as Waylon Jennings, Merle Haggard, and Willie Nelson. These collaborations have often resulted in highly acclaimed performances and recordings that have become staples of the country music canon. One particularly noteworthy collaboration was with Willie Nelson on the record "The Winning Hand" in 1982. This project brought together Kristofferson, Nelson, Dolly Parton, and Brenda Lee, showcasing the skills of four of country music's most distinctive voices. The album featured each artist singing solo as well as in various combinations, with Kristofferson's contributions highlighting his songwriting skills and his ability to harmonize with other strong singers.

Kristofferson's partnerships have not been limited to the country music world. He has worked with artists from different genres, showing his broad musical appeal and influence. For example, he worked with rock musician Bob Dylan on several occasions, including a memorable performance at Dylan's 30th Anniversary Concert Celebration in 1992. This event saw Kristofferson perform alongside a diverse array of artists, further cementing his place as a crossover star capable of appealing to multiple audiences. In the world of film, Kristofferson's collaborations have been equally impressive. He has worked with famous directors such as Martin Scorsese in "Alice Doesn't Live Here Anymore" (1974) and Sam Peckinpah in "Pat Garrett and Billy the Kid" (1973). These collaborations allowed Kristofferson to showcase his acting skills alongside his musical talents, working with some of the most respected figures in film.

Kristofferson's willingness to collaborate has also extended to younger artists, helping to introduce his music to new generations. He has performed and recorded with contemporary country stars such as Dierks Bentley and Jamey Johnson, bridging the gap between classic and modern country music. These collaborations have often involved performances of Kristofferson's classic songs, allowing newer artists to pay tribute to his legacy while introducing their own interpretations. In the late 1990s and early 2000s, Kristofferson participated in several tribute albums and concerts honoring his peers. These projects often involved collaborations with a wide range of artists from different genres. For example, he contributed to tribute albums for Johnny Cash, Waylon Jennings, and Willie Nelson, playing alongside artists from country, rock, and alternative music backgrounds. These collaborations not only celebrated the music of his friends and colleagues, but also showed Kristofferson's generation's enduring influence on popular music.

Kristofferson's collaborative spirit has also been obvious in his involvement with various charitable causes. He has participated in numerous benefit shows and recordings throughout his career, often working alongside other artists to raise awareness and funds for various social and environmental problems. These collaborations have allowed him to use his artistic platform for philanthropic purposes, further enhancing his reputation as not just a singer and actor but also as a socially conscious artist. One of his most intriguing collaborations came later in his career when he worked with producer Don Was on the album "This Old Road" in 2006. Was, known for his work with artists across various genres, helped to create an intimate, stripped-down sound that highlighted Kristofferson's songwriting and vocal performances. This collaboration resulted in one of Kristofferson's most highly acclaimed

late-career albums, demonstrating his continued
relevance and artistic growth. In recent years, he has
continued to work with a diverse array of artists. He has
performed in tribute concerts, guest spots on other artists'
albums, and special one-off performances that bring
together musicians from different generations and
genres. These collaborations have often served as a
reminder of Kristofferson's vast impact on American
music and his ability to connect with artists across the
musical spectrum.

 Kristofferson's collaborative work has also expanded to
the world of poetry and spoken word. He has
participated in events that mix music and poetry,
working with poets and writers to explore the
connections between songwriting and other forms of
literary expression. These collaborations have
highlighted the poetic quality of Kristofferson's lyrics
and his status as a songwriter whose work transcends
standard genre boundaries. Throughout his career, he has
shown a remarkable ability to change his style to
complement his collaborators while keeping his

distinctive artistic voice. Whether working with country music legends, rock stars, actors, or younger artists, he has consistently brought a level of sincerity and artistry to his collaborations that have enriched both his own work and that of his partners. His collaborative spirit has not only produced a wealth of memorable music and performances but has also played a major role in shaping his legacy. Through his willingness to work with artists from different backgrounds and generations, he has guaranteed that his music and impact will continue to reach new audiences. His collaborations have served as a bridge between different eras of popular music, helping to maintain the continuity of the American songwriting tradition.

Kris Kristofferson

CONCLUSION

Kristofferson has truly been a voice of his age, capturing the spirit of an era and expressing it through his art with unparalleled authenticity and depth. Kristofferson's road to success was far from straightforward. After graduating from Oxford as a Rhodes Scholar, he joined the Army, getting to the rank of captain. His transition from military life to the world of entertainment was fraught with challenges, including a time working as a janitor at Columbia Records while trying to make it as a songwriter. This phase of his life underscores another important lesson: perseverance in the face of adversity. Kristofferson's willingness to take on humble jobs while following his dreams serves as an inspiration to aspiring artists everywhere. Kristofferson, as a songwriter, revolutionized the country music genre. His lyrics, often highly personal and introspective, brought a new level of poetic sophistication to country music. Songs like "Me and Bobby McGee," "Help Me Make It Through the Night," and "Sunday Mornin' Comin' Down" not only became hits but also expanded the boundaries of what country music could say. These songs dealt with themes of freedom, loneliness, and the human condition in ways that resonate strongly with listeners. Kristofferson's ability to craft lyrics that were both deeply personal and universally relatable is a testament to his writing skill and deep understanding of the human experience.

His success as a songwriter paved the way for him in the world of music. As a recording artist, he added a raw, authentic voice to his music, which stood in stark contrast to the polished sound of mainstream country at the time. His gravelly vocals and unvarnished delivery perfectly complemented his introspective words, creating a unique sound that affected countless artists who followed. This authenticity in his performance style teaches us the value of staying true to one's artistic vision, even when it doesn't conform to industry standards. Kristofferson also found success as an actor, appearing in numerous films across several decades. His rugged attractive looks and natural charisma made him a compelling screen presence, but it was his willingness to take on difficult and varied roles that truly set him apart. From his Golden Globe-winning performance in "A Star Is Born" to his portrayal of an aging musician in "Blade," Kristofferson consistently showed his range and depth as an actor. His success in multiple artistic fields serves as a reminder of the power of versatility and the importance of continually challenging oneself artistically.

 Throughout his career, he has been known for his political activism and his commitment to social issues. He has used his platform to speak out on topics ranging from veterans' rights to environmental conservation. This aspect of his life teaches us about the responsibility that comes with fame and the potential for artists to effect positive change in the world. Kristofferson's activism reminds us that art can be a powerful tool for raising awareness and inspiring action on important social problems. His partnerships with other artists have been a hallmark of his career. His work with fellow country music legends Johnny Cash, Waylon Jennings, and Willie Nelson as part of The Highwaymen supergroup created some of the most memorable music of the 1980s and '90s. These collaborations not only resulted in outstanding art but also created a sense of community and mutual support among artists. This aspect of Kristofferson's career shows the value of collaboration and the magic that can happen when talented individuals come together in pursuit of a shared creative vision.

One of the most striking aspects of Kristofferson's work is his longevity. Despite the changing trends in popular music, he has stayed relevant and respected for over five decades. This enduring appeal is a testament to the timeless quality of his songwriting and the universal themes he tackles in his work. It also speaks to his ability to evolve as an artist while keeping true to his core artistic identity. This balance between growth and consistency is a valuable lesson for any creative professional seeking to build a lasting career. Kristofferson's journey also teaches us about the value of taking risks and embracing change. His choice to leave a promising military career to pursue music was a major gamble, as was his transition from songwriter to performer and actor. Each of these moves involved stepping out of his comfort zone and facing the possibility of failure. Yet it was these very risks that led to his greatest successes and allowed him to make his unique mark on American society.

Another key lesson from Kristofferson's life is the power of authenticity. Whether in his songwriting, his performances, or his public image, Kristofferson has always presented himself honestly and without pretense. This genuineness has endeared him to fans and won his peers' respect. In an industry often characterized by artifice and image manipulation, Kristofferson's dedication to being true to himself stands out as a refreshing and admirable quality. Kristofferson's career also shows the value of cross-pollination between different art forms. His work in music informed his acting, and vice versa, producing a rich, multifaceted artistic identity. This interdisciplinary approach not only broadened his creative horizons but also helped him reach diverse audiences. It serves as a reminder that creativity knows no limits and that artists can benefit greatly from exploring multiple forms of expression.

As we look back on Kristofferson's life and work, we see a man who has lived fully and authentically, using his talents to create art that speaks to the human condition in all its complexity. His songs have given solace, inspiration, and understanding to millions of listeners. His performances on screen have moved and entertained viewers around the world. Furthermore, his activism has given voice to important issues and inspired others to take action. In many ways, he embodies the spirit of his age: idealism, the questioning of authority, the search for personal freedom, and the desire to make the world a better place. But his appeal crosses generational boundaries. The honesty and emotional depth of his work continue to resonate with listeners of all ages, ensuring that his legacy will remain for generations to come. Kristofferson's legacy is not just in the songs he's written or the parts he's played, but in the lives he's touched and the artists he's inspired. He has shown us that it's possible to be both a great artist and a principled human being, to create work that is both personally meaningful and widely resonant. As we look to the future, we can be certain that Kris Kristofferson's impact will continue to be felt in music, film, and beyond, inspiring new generations of artists to find their voice and tell their stories with honesty, passion, and courage. Kris Kristofferson's life and work serve as a powerful reminder of the enduring impact of art that speaks truth to the human experience. His voice, in all its forms, has indeed been the voice of an age, and its echoes will continue to resonate for many generations to come.

Printed in Great Britain
by Amazon